3

We are inside the library.

We can see books.

We can see computers too.

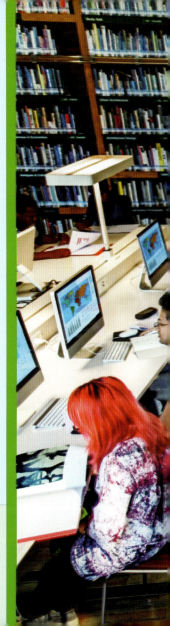

Here is a book on dinosaurs.

I can look inside this book.

Look at Mum and me.

We are looking for books.

Here is a book on flowers.

We can look inside this book.

Here is Mum.

Mum is looking for books too.

Here is a computer.

We can look for dinosaurs
on the computer.

We can look for flowers too.

Here is a big book.

I like this book.

I can look inside.

This is a good book
for me.

We like books!